JOHN STAMMERS read philosophy at King's College London and is an Associate of King's College. He was Judith E. Wilson Fellow at the University of Cambridge. His debut collection, *Panoramic Lounge-bar*, won the Forward Prize for Best First Collection. His second, *Stolen Love Behaviour*, was Poetry Book Society Choice and was shortlisted for the T.S. Eliot Prize. His third collection, *Interior Night*, was published by Picador in 2010. He has edited *The Picador Book of Love Poems* and a selection of Gerard Manley Hopkins' poems, published by Faber and Faber. He lives in Oxfordshire with his two sons, his partner and her daughter.

Also by John Stammers in Picador

Interior Night

Stolen Love Behaviour

Panoramic Lounge-bar

AS EDITOR

The Picador Book of Love Poems

John Stammers

Queries on Death, the Infinite and Irrational Numbers

PICADOR POETRY

First published 2025 by Picador
an imprint of Pan Macmillan
The Smithson, 6 Briset Street, London EC1M 5NR
EU representative: Macmillan Publishers Ireland Ltd, 1st Floor,
The Liffey Trust Centre, 117–126 Sheriff Street Upper,
Dublin 1 D01 YC43
Associated companies throughout the world

ISBN 978-1-0350-8268-1

Copyright © John Stammers 2025

The right of John Stammers to be identified as the
author of this work has been asserted in accordance with
the Copyright, Designs and Patents Act 1988.

All rights reserved. No part of this publication may be reproduced,
stored in a retrieval system, or transmitted, in any form, or by any means
(including, without limitation, electronic, mechanical, photocopying, recording
or otherwise) without the prior written permission of the publisher.

Pan Macmillan does not have any control over, or any responsibility for,
any author or third-party websites (including, without limitation, URLs,
emails and QR codes) referred to in or on this book.

1 3 5 7 9 8 6 4 2

A CIP catalogue record for this book is available from the British Library.

Printed and bound in the UK using 100% Renewable Electricity by CPI Group (UK) Ltd

This book is sold subject to the condition that it shall not, by way of trade or otherwise,
be lent, hired out, or otherwise circulated without the publisher's prior consent in any form
of binding or cover other than that in which it is published and without a similar condition
including this condition being imposed on the subsequent purchaser. The publisher does not
authorize the use or reproduction of any part of this book in any manner for the purpose of
training artificial intelligence technologies or systems. The publisher expressly reserves
this book from the Text and Data Mining exception in accordance with Article 4(3)
of the European Union Digital Single Market Directive 2019/790.

Visit **www.picador.com** to read more about all our books and to buy them.

for Suzanne

Contents

Street Scene with Balloon 1

Funeral II 2

Thursday Twentieth of February 3

The Beach 4

The Real Names of Things 5

A Prospect of Duck End in November 6

States 7

I Celebrate the World's Next Birthday 9

Girl in a Scarlet Wig Watches a Man Change a Wheel from an Upstairs Window 10

Poem on the Lid of a Shoebox 11

Queries on Death, the Infinite and Irrational Numbers with Miroslav Holub and Occasional Kitten 14

Death Songs 17

Autumn Thoughts on a Train 29

Just for Now 31

Morning Love 32

Lure 33

Girl Sitting at the Back of a Motor Boat   35

October with Pigeons   36

Cantata   37

Meditation on a Question of Love   39

The Leveret   40

There are Ways of Being Together   42

Leaving the Club   43

The House-Sit   45

All the Words   46

Acknowledgements   51

Queries on Death, the Infinite and Irrational Numbers

Street Scene with Balloon

I walked down my childhood street; I saw my enemy.
It made me think of rotted daffodils.
She turned a smile and blew me a kiss.
I smiled in return and laughed towards her.

There were unknown people with dogs that ran there.
The trees began an odd dance in the loose spring air
and the pale blossom played in the daylight like children
on a picnic where cakes and jelly are expected.

Once, when I was a small child at play in that street,
a man who had the features of my father approached me.
He said he was my older self inside his own memory of the day
he met a tall man in that street who resembled my father.

As I drew near my enemy, a yellow party-balloon
grew outwards from my upper body, large and larger.
The street I walked down – my street –
the thin screech of a fingernail on the taut skin of a balloon –

she became further away – I – again as she approached –
further – I did not know who I could be – scream   who
she was nothing – no one – I reached my enemy,
we embraced. I saw a small boy playing. The day burst.

Funeral II

Your collected works are all here
together in the one volume:
the Queen of Cups, the extrovert in his hiding,
the boy left to make sense of sense.

The cold rectangle of the chapel
is the sarcophagus of our loss;
the catafalque supports
our northern sky.

Four years have passed, four years
since the final periodicity of your line:
the permanent flowering of your bonny new status.

You were a charm, my dear Roderick,
but charm is a meagre lustre
wiped away with a wave of the damned.

Thursday Twentieth of February

The blue fervour of eleven o'clock occasions a vague thoughtfulness,
the unclouded February daylight the more so,
whereas last evening was so sharply awake in sexual concentration:
the ego is a bodily ego, which is to say the body has purposes
the body knows not of. So much and so little of an hour
passes notice or, more precisely, may come to be noticed
within another, different hour. Just as the hour
we spent in recombination too long in the not being
is available now in this present now –
your pupils' fathomless swell, their oceanic pull –
it serves to bring back again, now again, over again
that which may be missed, but nonetheless regained in the review.
In the same way that a morning of sky-blue cold
is held in light of an absolute intelligence,
unconcerned and implacable, call it what you will.

The Beach

for J and F

Your childhoods will soon be closed like the ice-cream kiosk
of our heart-quick summers, and everything now will be then.

I see you there on the beach at Studland on our last day
as the sun blazes its azimuth across the clifftop to its finale.

My arms reach with the want to draw you back there —
both knelt at your newly-dug abyss which the tide will soon fill up

and my two men gaze downwards into the blank unknown
of what there is to follow, what is to be found out,

your faces alight with a new idea: that you can dig
far enough to prevent it, to stop what cannot be postponed.

The Real Names of Things

The real names of things are hidden from us.
The dragonfly is green daylight through a rippled pane
or filaments of green gold from a lamé dress
whilst its inner self remains inviolate and shut.

Too much is known as exterior impressions,
too much for the blue jay's feather to overbear
upon our partial comprehensions
so shatters to nameless blue fragments.

I fear that, in my narrow concern,
I have encountered merely the exemplar
of things in the world,
like an eclipse viewed though the slit in a card.

The flower is more violet in frost.
This affects my sensibility
with something like a shock —
surfaces have their depths.

So I carry a form of anguish to know
such exquisite, imminent matter,
the anonymous modalities,
the name the tiger calls the tiger.

A Prospect of Duck End in November

The flight of a green woodpecker —
the landscape is its mind
that runs green and sensational through its vision.

The considerate painter brings oils and powder pigments
with his special mode of apprehension and practical thought.
The palette of full sight is the bidden heart.

With consummate delicacy,
like the sudden vale's misty net,
the canvas accepts the paint:

a vermilion berry on a green hedge,
grey strokes on the brush-wash ground
bound by the conceit. Heart care as heart.

States

The feel of a past lays its uncanny hands on me.
Perhaps it has travelled across this gold New England bay,
its pleasure boats and modest, glammy summer homes.
Then again, maybe it's not the past but the distance.
Such was my manic drive along the multivarious landscapes
in rough pursuit of some necessary point
somewhere before the world's wide shore:
town-after-towns noted only for what they produce
or the grimy diversions of their nightlifes.
Their hardcore industrialism
was no match for my perpetual good humour.
No one is more resolutely cheery than a man
with a firm grasp of his own mortality –
shake hands, old son, with nothing whatsoever:
there's quite a lot of it.
                    Alas, though, that's just halfway
to nowhere in particular, and here I am
in some Gloucester Mass. of the apprehension,
so far east it must be the Atlantic waters
that have run down my face and left their residue
in fine salty lines, and I can all but taste London.
But if I'm anywhere it must be west, a long way west,
way out beyond the black sands
and the bleached dead steers and the sage brush,
maybe in that clearing on the pine-wood coast,
bad tempered by now, dry-mouthed and belligerent,

as the Pacific's wide stare meets my own
and I trample the dry needles under my feet.
If I listen closely, I can almost hear me.

I Celebrate the World's Next Birthday

From almost the window's edge
calls a song thrush
in its prial
of melodies

the sharp crusts thrust out
as if to say
Pythagoras
noticed us

but I see the icing on the cake
dancing in glucose-dosages
as white as teeth
and here is eternity in a teacup

as the leaf-heavy trees swarm
above the tick-tock tick-tock lawn

Girl in a Scarlet Wig Watches a Man Change a Wheel from an Upstairs Window

for T

The festive season has brought forth all manner of blossom:
the holly berries are drops of stage-blood around the porch,
the crazi-hair wig like its own nervous breakdown,
the bust tyre on the Dodge Ram pick-up in the driveway.
The check-shirted stepfather glares into the toolbox and reddens
as if in some chromatic sympathy with the wig;
the sweat stain down the back of his shirt
could be the Delaware crossing Washington.
Cars have wheels, wheels have cars,
she, though, has an important point to make,
leans out the window and calls into the kringley night,
her words frozen to white cotton-candy in mid-beseech.
She gives up soon enough, falls silent,
Miss Yankee-Hairdo-of-the-Year,
or the Scarlet Rose of Massachusetts,
but the wig, the wig is incessant.

Poem on the Lid of a Shoebox

i.m. James Aubrey

'The best Tom ever'
         — Tennessee Williams

I time-slipped into an era last night: it was a long time ago,
but not so far you can't get there from here
because memory is the shortest distance between places.
So it wasn't that hard for me to get there after all.
I should have died any number of times since,
but it turns out I was more attached to life
than I ever thought I would be.
I've outlived the old stories —
perhaps I just needed to see what happened at the end.

So when I switched on a rare TV channel,
I was back in my basement living-room again,
back to when you were your real self,
to the days when *A Bouquet of Barbed Wire* was a cultural scandal.
And each week there would always be another shock,
another tabloid sensation: would they? wouldn't they?
his daughter, the mother-in-law? For fuck's sake!

I never slept with Prue or Cassie. I was looking for my life
somewhere in the addled discord of the seventies.
Our birthdays fell on the same date, brothers under a sun sign —
strange how it comes round the same time every year.
In those days, I was your cause and you were my célèbre;
foolishness makes us love, love makes us foolish.

November seventy-nine: you were the one
who drove the long hour through London daybreak
to tell me my father had died in the night.
The hardest speech you ever had to make, you said.
Later that week, you sped us down to the south coast
in your red minivan, *The Sun Sessions*
rocking and rolling over the tapeheads
and us singing 'Blue Moon of Kentucky'.

I looked out across the Solent then turned to you.
I have that photo still: late sun on the wave tops.
My face is hard with three-day-old defiance,
my hair cascadent and Doorsy about my shoulders,
eyes glistened with salt. If you'd looked like me,
you said, you could have played James Bond.
You had class, you could have been an Oscar winner,
but characters live forever, not so child actors.
You just weren't able to keep it going,
to blow into the conch, to hold your note
at that beautiful, starry pitch.

Jimmy, none of us are young any more,
and you're not even here. The old locals
are closing down in Islington and Notting Hill.
And the truth is, my birthday ghost,
I have grown innocent since my younger days,

that guileful resentment and chagrin
merely the posture of a world-weariness,
and the pains and perturbations of my youth
seem to me now like passing images
on a screen: over-dramatised and banal.
You see, that young man, young joker,
is a memory-construct from the days
when our lives were the undated future.

So, if I walk past one of the ancient haunts,
which I rarely do, and the sweat of stale beer
on pub carpets catches in my memory,
I see you throw back your head
with that methodical laugh of yours,
truer than real, and once more it all begins
to spool through my head, to play out
in the terrible, dissonant flicker of horizontal lines
like the late-night rerun of an old TV drama
that once shocked a nation, but whose leading actors
you just can't put a name to.

Queries on Death, the Infinite and Irrational Numbers with Miroslav Holub and Occasional Kitten

So Miroslav Holub said that we should not fear Dying for, at the point of Death, our trusty Endocrine System floods our bodies with all the endorphins it has to flood with.

So that we really do go out on a High.

So remember he told us the best way to kill a Kitten was to cut its Head off with a pair of Kitchen Scissors?

So he Knew a thing or two about Death.

So what if it turned out that at the instant of Death your Inner Experience was really of your Whole Life just racing right past you?

What if during that last instant of Heady Rush, it is also the case that, in your Experience of your Consciousness, you relive said Life the same over and over, but in smaller and smaller amounts of Real Time, because our Subjective Experience is no respecter of Time? Just ask Dreams.

So what if it's like one of Zeno's Paradoxes?

So that your Life recurs to you again and again Without End like an Irrational Number or Pi or whichever one you favour?

So that we just keep going through an Infinite Amount of Lives you can't get to the end of because they get smaller and smaller, but that you don't Experience it getting smaller and smaller, because our Subjective Experience is no respecter of Time, after all? Just ask Dreams (q.v.)

So what if Memory were a hole, an aperture you look through to an Event that is happening Now, like a Scene or Tableau seen out of the window of a train you're on?

What if maybe it's like a really fast Adlestrop?
So that you know its Characters and Street Furniture and Oblique
    Angled Shadows so you feel it really is there and you say to
    yourself 'It really is there!'?
So what if Recurring is just another way of saying Keep
    Happening, which it is?
So what if the Leisure Principle, which I have just coined, is where
    a person turns whatever they have into Leisure even if it's not
    Leisure?
So what if the reason my Father cared about work so much was
    because he didn't have any Leisure?
So that my Father found Leisure at work with his Attractive
    Workmate?
So what if that Now of infinitely recurring Death moments is an
    unending, sub-divided range of the same old damned things
    like the Day my Father left to go and live with his Attractive
    Workmate?
So what if Saved or Damned is same thing anyway?
What if Religion falls in the face of the Infinite?
What if when In Extremis you really do live your Life over and
    over in diminishing Time Slices so that no one, not even your
    Nearest and Dearest, God Love Them, stood in a Solemn Tableau
    around your bed, would know?
So what if This Life Now is one of those Infinite Number of
    repeated lives, but you could Never Tell because it's the same
    By Definition?
What if Déjà Vu is a Minute Glimpse of that past first real life
    poking through?
What if that is what's meant by an Infinite Regress?
So what if the line out of that poem which says

'I was able to see we'd both regressed', is Really True, but for All of Us?

So what if, if we could but see it, it looks like that Production Line of mirrors 'nested mirror within mirror' but which is just two mirrors, one set against the other?

So what if I am one mirror and my Death is the other?

So that we look at each other with Infinite Puzzlement?

So that if mirrors could speak they would say 'What the?'

What if the Light between the mirrors just gets a little less every Iteration?

So that it gets a little Darker every time?

So what if it Fades?

What if it really is a Fading of the Light?

So what if you would never know because Each Next Life appears to you at least as brightly lit as itself?

So what if it doesn't apply to Kittens?

What if it's all about Endorphins and Light?

Imagine that. Life.

Death Songs

I

I don't expire often, but if I do
eminent surgeons crowd in,
anaesthetists prepare exotic gasses and potions,
operating theatres are rigged with vast lamps.
        — A scene, Johnnyboy, to grace
          a glossy medical journal.
A multi-page feature, at the very least.
        — Your native recalcitrance stood you in good stead.
A convenient trait. I wielded it with no little grace.

   Lower his temperature to 18 °C, please

        — How did you busy yourself in the long hours?
I encouraged the mortuary staff   not at all.
        — I have seldom known you so crazed.
Your judgement is kindly, if somewhat off-beam.
        — And went the performance well,
          in this theatre of living parts?

   He appears revived, somewhat.

The whole ensemble was amazed.
They disrobed with a grand flourish,
genuflected to the god of sutures
and resolved
never to operate again . . .
        — So what of Johnnyboy?

I found myself completely elsewhere.

II

I lay in my own corpse and passed the time of day,
moribund but not inactive: my internal landscapes ranged
the mauve confections of Claude Lorraine and Poussin
Et in coma ego.

An induced state is a further realm, further than R.E.Ms,
further, where the wanderer goeth without let or restraint.
Consciousness is, after all, the capacity to undergo a delusion.
        – If you say so. You are out there today.

    Please check his O2 levels . . .

When burst in a hierophant clad in robes of bronze tulle.
He demanded a pedestal upon which to declaim.
I swept my good arm at the dais I had concocted.
        – A gracious and kindly gesture, Johnnyboy,
          given his peremptory behaviour thus far.
I am the acme of genteel.
He damned me, thrice, then vanished.
        – So much for good manners.
The Möbius ribbon of my oddball day flipped once more,
preparatory for the next stage in my onward static voyage
whence no traveller.

    His breathing is weak but stabilized

Meanwhile, I respired in accordance with the pump:
chest in, in, in out, out, out,
the awful seconds,
in, in, in out, out, out . . .

III

Unprepared for the joyless ecstasy of the dead zone,
I became aware in my unconsciousness of others.
They were slouched upright in corners and against walls,
their heads bowed onto their chests.

>*He is restless, he is reaching for something*

They were like the dead souls of mannequins
who had seen their last shop window.
>– And who might you say these others were?

I knew them and their exhibited lack of eagerness.
Remote cousins of my beloved
from country parts,
they had concocted a realm of their own, no doubt,
in which I, in my turn, was a shop-depleted mannequin
slumped to the floor splayed-legged and inert.

>*We must turn him . . . he appears in some discomfort*

Far-off words flowed to the sound of minor instruments,
no sense could I discern.

>– So how did you resolve the matter?

My friend, I determined to nap until oblivion.

IV

I was a wanderer of the Lower Indo-Gangetic Plain
astride my Triumph Bonneville T120
sometime in the late sixth century BCE.
      – I never took you for a biker,
       if I have to be truthful.

I drew across and stopped by the side of the road
where sat a deadbeat who told me his name was Siddhartha Gautama.
He had been there for the last forty-seven days without food
or drink.
      – Not even a Domino's for delivery or a can of Diet Pepsi?
Not even a ripened fig fallen from an adjacent fig tree.

Do you seek? asked Siddhartha Gautama
as he swung onto the Bonnie's pillion like he owned the place.
      – He was interested in you, I think,
       to so self-assuredly mount the steed.
Without doubt.

Brother, I ride where the wheels spin me
towards the final enlightenment that is death, I said,
through the side of my mouth
in order for him to fully catch my words.

I will travel with you a way, said Siddhartha Gautama
as we sped along beside the Ganges at a mighty clip,
you seem to know what you're talking about.

V

It occurs to me that, our noted confabulations
notwithstanding,
I have never told you how I became Johnnyboy.
       – A transformation wholly to be guessed.
       I have often hypothesised, to no real purpose.

In my naïve years they would hail me a plain John,
in order, no doubt, to provide a lightweight with a little gravity.
       – And this expedient, how went it?
Merely the nomenclature of seriousness did I besport.
       – So what happened to prise this label from you?
       A sticky problem if there ever was.

I pitched myself down a huge flight of stairs
where there was no staircase
only floor.
The dead weight of the iron Earth
came up to collide
with my future dead self. Or so it thought.

I saw nary a star   nary a bright planetoid . . .
       – I am, if you will permit the term, dying
       to hear what became of you.
Flat out, I lay there for weeks.

       – And your name, what of your name?
Being therefore more worldly than my earlier self,
they were compelled
to call me by a younger soubriquet.

VI

I never considered myself to have much of a chance
of surviving life.
So, when I woke up asleep
in the middle of dying
I was not at all surprised. *Au contraire*,
I was, yes, enchanted:
multitudes of high-toned gongs sounded faint and pure,
and a bronze monochrome pervaded all.
A succulent deliciousness, felt I.
— So what then, Johnnyboy, did you, in fact, die?

It was all too obvious to me
that I was in a fluxacious stream of mind bound not for glory
but nowhere.
— You are eloquent beyond comprehension.
Death wants what death wants, I say.

John, wake up

I must stress,
the process of dying does not prepare one for death.

John, wake up, you have been very unwell

But it was then I felt an electrophysical touch
like a query I had no answer for:
life had not finished with me yet;
there was some more of it.

VII

Claiming to be a medical professional of sorts,
in the small hours it was, she appeared to me
a dextrous avatar of Lakshmi attired in scrubs and lanyard.

I told her my wish was of necessity to relieve myself –
my bladder-need was expansive, my wretched clenched teeth –
and that I must rise from the slab and walk,
the far distant toilet-room a destination
beyond which I could not conceive . . .
        – O Johnnyboy. I feel your predicament!

This is *forbidden*, she said,
not lacking a certain relish
in the saying of it, I thought.
        – And how did you respond?

Catheterised as I was, I felt nothing but shame.
Free me, I cried silently, but without a tear.

Do you know where you are? she said.
Always confident in this type of situation,
I answered her in my teeth,
Yes, I am in the night ward in Oxford.
Not at all, she breathed, you are in *Wales*.

VIII

One fine autumn morn, I awoke in the intensive care unit
to a novel perspective.
       – You find appeal
           in the most unpromising of situations.

I encountered there one Charles Bonnet.
He peered out
from a pair of bulbous yellow spectacles
like the wild wag of an oculist of American fable.
       – You saw this?

With my one mental eye. Or, to be precise, not him
but, preferable by far, his syndrome.
       – And what may that be, this syndrome eponymous?

It was fauxtastical:
a cataract of clinicians, all white-coated and in fractal degree,
descended 'gainst a verdant ground, backlit by fluorescence.
       – I like the sound of this, Johnnyboy,
          such jollity for the time of day!

The vibrations of the electromagnetic spectrum
decorated my visual field
like the kitsch diorama of a taxidermalogical display
or the feature wallpaper of a house
in a recently gentrified neighbourhood.
       – Striking once, then nauseating thereafter.

Autumn Thoughts on a Train

The leaves in turn, a patina of hammered bronze,
cling to their dark matrix of branches,
and I am shaken as they rush past
as if they, not I, were going anywhere.
I am on a train bound for a certain terminus
when I catch a half-sight of a figure in the glass
and see that it is you, Wallace Stevens.

Grey haired sensualist in a business suit,
meticulous in matters of intellectual taste,
you are the brilliant uncle I never had.
You had the plain good sense I failed to acquire,
worked behind a desk and settled insurance claims
for unfortunates burned out of their Connecticut houses,
foiled false claimants in their fraudulent shenanigans
and took the five forty-two home each night.

Installed by a congenial carriage window
you watched the American dream stream past you
in the evening colours of a New England fall
and found the seat of the imagination moved with it
past every halt, small town and crossing
while you penned gaudy stanzas
from your lavish, synoptic mind,
and fixed ordinary occurrences to a permanent oddness.

Moquette upholstery in a panelled compartment –
to find strange beauty in one's own apprehension
is a spectacular calling,
an astringent sanity that travels beyond its origin
like a line of blue smoke in a white cloud.
Let us make poetry from the manufactured world
of locomotives, railway signs and signal lamps.

I turn and move as the train moves.
The wheels pulse their well-worn rhythm
through us as we head towards the final stop.
Since I died, I no longer revere you above me,
for death is the one true leveller under any aesthetic;
closer than that, *mon oncle*, I would sit beside you.

Just for Now

for Jess on her birthday

Just for now, as the blue canopy of the sky
drifts away from us
and, I know you'll understand,
the defunct geraniums,
remnant shells of colours and breaths taken,

stand where their lives once were,
isn't it strange that the light finds us both
at the same instant and you ask
if I think the summer is over
now that the geraniums have gone.

They must have left, I said,
before you arrived that year,
leaving you to inhale the flowerless air
between cries and cries – and in time
there will be more of those, so many!

But right now, everything is a sundial
as the long hand of autumn shadow
points to the moment and we stand
prior to the next breath,
prior to the next.

Morning Love

Who have no soft nights nor warm afternoons
must peradventure try their loves in earlier hours.
The daylight sharp and inflexible,
they lie in cooled sheets and hear outside
the energetic day happen past their window.
Yet they find in that dislocated moment,
before the tyranny of midday
and the passing embrace of goodbyes,
a more determined lovemaking
loosed of cliché, habit or resignation,
a kind only to be committed in full need,
pressed to the morning and akin to rage.

Lure

i.m. Raymond Carver

The fish followed you up the river,
right from the beginning they followed you,
from the shallows to the rapids, the breakneck stones,
to the deep basins and rock pools
and higher still to the waterfall.

They were there in those nights
when you dreamt of the young grilse.
Did you dream they would one day leap
into your arms like the final gust of wind
into the arms of a high-wire artist?

Fish shadowed you to the dusk of a sea-boat trip
when the mouth of a huge dog shark
gaped open at you from the depths like a howl,
bit through your line as if it were floss
and shook you like a premonition.

Deep inside everything is a memory of a self:
I once saw the glaze of a live fish
sliced into; they excised its heart
but it continued to beat on a dish,
driving on and onwards and on;

the sockeye return to their spawning-grounds —
the high, montane reaches,
the glassy, freshwater courses —
and even the cool river-bed rocks conceal
what sustains them.

At last you find a way up to the waterfall.
You make your one cast into its pool;
your line pierces the froth like a steel wire,
hooks onto something below, some dark shadow
that moves through the inevitable waters.

Finally you land it, which has come to land you,
approach it uncertainly like a stranger,
and ask yourself and almost remember
what mission beats in that other as you take it
in two heavy hands and weigh its secret.

Girl Sitting at the Back of a Motor Boat

for C

The colour sense of it could only be Matisse:
the inarticulate shiver of the sea's spilled petrol,
the sky chill as pale-blue eyes.
Her crimson fleece jacket clashes arbitrarily
with her gingery hair
and the white water-spray that licks
the powerful boat's cream outline.
Her back is turned.
The gulls fly out their erratic parabolas
and temporary screeches
as she keeps her still counsel.
She is fourteen.
She sits and observes the wake.
She waits for life to start.

October with Pigeons

A line of pigeons squat on top of a streetlight.
It is the end of the day and the sun has been benign this year;
it has hung on to remind everyone that summer has really been.
Only the extended shadows of late daylight tell-tale
the end of the sunny days. They are not of the wild, these squabs, no,
they are indubitably urban. They could be passengers on the tube,
a group of silent and brooding commuters in their uniform grey suits,
motionless now at the end of a hard day
pecking up unexpected delicacies and defecating on the public statuary.
It is a question whether they are grateful
for the sun's afterthought, these feathered brethren of the lamp-post.
If anything registers in them of the simple feel of heat on the back
in the company of one's kind, then perhaps they are.
Many of them will not survive the winter.
Their reason is too now for them to meditate on a hereafter,
but they can bask in the last beams of this here, this now.

Cantata

after Juan Gil-Albert

When you were a fragile ingenue –
your pale unblemished neck
and clear white skin in the daylight of Toledo –
the beat of bird-flight and burst of petals
opened under the sky. I saw then
all that your look could contain
and wrote you living poems.

I see along my memories it was there
you fixed me with your sea-dark gaze
which shook me like the sudden birds
and the esoteric blooms.
In our cool siesta, I trailed my hand
through your hair and felt the waves
of a subtle lagoon where desire holds.

From this advance of my life
I see, in that first conjoin,
past the sway of ferns and wild palms
to the fragrant iterations of roses
and the scent-bright days that are gone:
the stock that flowered them
now a grey and permanent shade.

Your vital colours have never changed.
The face of the one I now see
bears that beauty which does not change
despite the earthly grey
or the last wing-beat
that would carry us beyond the borders
of our contemplatable earth.

Find me, instead, at this other remove
where I view my lifetime of days.
Turn your wine-dark tears to me, former young woman
whose hair may still invoke the wander of breezes,
the excitement of youth and journey.
Now I lay out vines of saturated sweetness
along the openness of their fields.

To see each other joined again as lovers
and the vinescapes of that earth,
the full vineyards that offer up
the tastes and aromas of fertile expanse,
is as a sensual Toledo night in which
we hold to the warm air's breath that holds us.
Those sweet fruits are for you more than roses.

Meditation on a Question of Love

The grey moonscape, the black sky,
the wind cool across the ground;
I look over the land, blink at the dark,
everywhere a standstill, the earth turned night.

You asked me a question; I respond in kind.
What is it you ask me, you with a mouth
full of question marks and wild assumptions
that there is an answer? Love?

The dream-crossed lovers that work and sleep
for the most part simply live their unjustified loves.
The dispassionate night, not unsure but unaskable,
passes without clamour, asks no definition.

The semi-lit fields of the normal hours of early day
are comprehensible and assured, breathe light.
We walk together in an uncommon way
not to know what will prolong this walk of ours.

The Leveret

August 2023

As I walked out into the warm, free air
in the top lane, by the verge, I came across,
still as a stone slate,
a young hare, a juvenile, half grown.
What damage or contusion it had undergone
I cannot say to stay immobile at my approach,
still as a stone slate,
where it lay and waited for its time
in sudden, fatal gasps.
It suffered me, though, to lift it to my arms
where, in sudden, fatal gasps,
it lay and waited for its time.

Its fur ran beneath my hand
like a golden wheatfield
in the late-summer wind.
I stroked its leonine head
in the late-summer wind
like a golden wheatfield,
looked into its profound black eye
and saw there not an answer
but a portent,
I looked into its profound black eye
and saw there a shadow
thrown not by light but by darkness.

I laid it down upon its one good side
where, all in the one place,
it galloped its long stride –
freed from its broken self, fugitive and wild,
as if over the meadows and the running brook,
all in the one place,
it coursed in pursuit of its own young life.
Until, at last, it reached the end
of the dream-fields and imagined hedgerows;
until in pursuit of its own young life
it reached the end of its putative flight
not an inch further on from where it was placed.

The one true beauty I should ever know
was about to leave the world of days
and so pass this creature of wonders;
my sweet companion of the hour
was about to leave the world of days.
To be truly of the world
is to care for it for the right reasons.
I closed its muzzle in my fist,
spoke douce blandishments
into its silken ear –
its closed muzzle in my fist,
I held my breath and waited.

There are Ways of Being Together

On those open clifftops of the northerly zones,
in outsized superstructures and avian idiosyncrasies,
the albatross mate their one mate.
In the long rapture of pairing-off for rearing
they emerge a side-on reflection of one another
to paso doble and beat each other about the head
with staccato, yellow bills.
The union gives up a single, giant egg,
white and plain as a bone china bowl.
Each tends to it with unhurried attention.
They place the warm down
of their alternate abdomens upon it.
At such elevations they watch for the other
in the overall sky or a signal grey and white smear
on the ocean's undecidable texture,
their whole being turned
towards an expectation, this, the next.

Leaving the Club

I step up from the basement café
and leave the early evening below
in the cellar bar where I have just read my poems.
I leave with it the implicit self-sense
of who I was that wrote them.
I stroll past banks of eateries
that fire out hot air into the street.
I pass two young queens in full drag.
They make spectacular gestures
towards a rank of taxi-drivers
who compare anecdotes
over polystyrene cups of street tea.
This is Soho on a heated-up evening:
the downright openness of the place,
the straight sleaze if you will.
I have met myself in a different life here.
The rain-moist pavement is flanked with blue neon;
my feet sink into its buoyant surface
as I move past restaurant fronts
with their window-seat couple scenarios.
I imagine myself as the young Marlowe
as he walked the city in the rain,
the dark and the light, steam and heat.
Seen through the eyes of someone else
this place is a fiction, I think,
when, from just behind me,
the louche young queens sweep past,

one of them runs a gloved hand across my shoulder.
I would descend into the tube,
make my way to the other side of town
and the plain habitations of everyday life,
but the walk back to Leicester Square
at the end of this testament of evenings –
the lights ice-blue on the asphalt, the open doors –
has caught me up in reflections
that crowd into me along the streets:
who I am and with what attention I live.

The House-Sit

I found the third the most difficult.
The owner had written a note-to-self
to direct them towards the radio.

A toothless breadknife lay across
a rutted board covered with the crumbs
of ancient sandwiches and long-dead toast.

The garden door was labelled GARDEN DOOR.
Whereas the only way out
was through a set of old French windows.

In the irregular tappings that emanated
from the pantry wall and clothes cupboards,
I could discern the sad plaints of captive spirits.

A split in the lead flashing above
had let errant rainwater bring forth
a fur of mycelium in the airing cupboard.

With every breath of those other people's air
came the thin, alien odour,
sweet and adhesive, of bodies lived and died in.

Observed through a pane of dull glass on the landing,
the night clouds shifted like grey milk in water.
There was never a moon to speak of.

All the Words

I have used up all the words.
Perhaps they have gone to their subtle niches
to secret themselves this sunstruck day, day of brightness and heat;
shadow seekers they have become,
crevice dwellers of the new apocalypse of verse.
Or do I revile? Am I an arch reviler?
I have never thought of myself as such, but who does?
O so many questions I have in the front of my mind.
Get back, you scoundrels of inquisitiveness!
I need to cogitate, to sift and sort.
As if I have the answers, *moi!*
a simple aesthete with a shameful taste for the ugly:
those mid-century modern veneers,
Murano glasswares and mannerist portraits –
Madonna with the Long Neck how you draw my eye!
If only I could come by a hammock
and lie in a breezy sway like a Black Mountain poet
and compose free verse paeans to pinewoods and creeks.
Or maybe meander on down a boulevard,
complaisant and smiley as a Beat,
until my sandals give way and I fall

Yet the beginning of me is not the now of me
and the last of me will go without warning
will go to where I have not been
to where the others are gone
my others, resolved into no more
than fabulous tales of who they were
insubstantial but full of human traits
as figures from a sacred dream time
who have become myth

Acknowledgements

Some poems in this collection have previously been published in *Bad Lilies* and *The Poetry Review*.

The two quotations in the poem 'Queries on Death . . .' are from 'The House Swap' by Allan Crosbie and 'Black Ice and Rain' by Michael Donaghy respectively. 'Cantata' is a version of 'Himno a la Vida' by Juan Gil-Albert. The title 'Poem on the Lid of a Shoebox' is taken from Tom's speech at the end of 'The Glass Menagerie' by Tennessee Williams.

Numerous people have helped and supported me in recent years; foremost amongst them are: Neil Hounsell, Jacquie Campbell, Mick Herbert, Wendy Slater, Araminta Morris, Beatrice Garland, David Taylor, Edward Barker, Barbara Marsh, Fiona Wright, Mike Wright, Stuart Paterson, Kathryn Gray, and Andrew Neilson.

I would like to thank Colette Bryce for her criticism, advice and encouragement.

I need to extend my undying gratitude to everyone at the Cardiothoracic Unit at the John Radcliffe Hospital, Oxford, in particular my surgeon Priya Sastry. I also would like to say a thank you to all at the Stroke Unit at the John Radcliffe.

I want to say a loving thank you to my two sons, Jay and Freddie, for being there for me when I needed them and in my recovery.

Lastly, I need to express how grateful I am to my partner, Suzanne Dean, for her love, dedication and unwavering support, without which this collection could not have been written.